nickelodeon™

TEENAGE MUTANT NINJA ™

TURTLES

KRAANG ATTACK!

Popcorn
ELT
Readers

Meet ...
everyone from

nickelodeon
TEENAGE MUTANT NINJA TURTLES ™

The Teenage Mutant Ninja Turtles live under New York City.

All the Turtles have ninja stars.

Leonardo

Michelangelo

Donatello

Raphael

Kraangdroid

The Kraang are aliens. They live in Kraangdroids.

Snake

Snake works for the Kraang.

Kraang

This is mutagen. Mutagen turns people and animals into mutants. ......o

This is the Kraang's Lair.

Splinter

Splinter is the Turtles' teacher or *sensei*.

April

April lives in New York. The Kraang have April and her dad at their lair.

Before you read ...
What do you think?
The Turtles want to help April. What is their plan?

New Words

What do these new words mean? Ask your teacher or use your dictionary.

helicopter

The **helicopter** is fast.

alien

Look! It's an **alien**!

hit

Hit it!

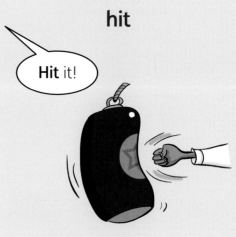

drive

She's **driving**.

plan

Let's make a **plan**!

ready

I'm **ready**!

turn into

She **turned into** a black cat.

roof

The cat's on the **roof**.

van

It's an old **van**.

shoot

Don't **shoot**!

'Get him!'

Get him!

Verbs

Present	Past
drive	drove
fall	fell
shoot	shot

What does the title *Kraang Attack!* mean? Ask your teacher.

CHAPTER ONE
'Who makes the mutagen?'

'Why are we here?' asked Mikey.

It was night in New York and the Turtles waited and watched.

'We want to find April,' said Leo. 'Someone down there knows something.'

A van drove into the road.

'Yes!' said Leo. 'Let's go and ask that man.'

The Turtles jumped down.

'Stop!' Raph shouted to the man.

'There are four of us and one of you,' said Donnie. 'So what are you going to do?'

The man shot at the Turtles and drove away.

'Oh no!' shouted Raph to Donnie. 'Why did you ask that?'

'Get him!' shouted Leo.

The Turtles ran across the roofs. Raph jumped down onto the van. But it didn't stop and Raph fell off. Leo hit the van with his ninja star.

CRASH!

'Now we've got him!' said Leo.

The Turtles ran quickly to the van. Raph opened the door and something blue fell out.

'Wow!' said the Turtles.

'This is mutagen,' said Donnie.

'We know all about mutagen,' said Leo. 'It's in Splinter's story.'

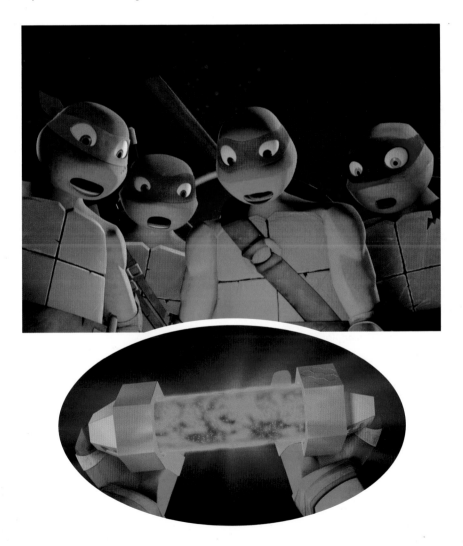

Fifteen years ago Splinter was a young man. One night he walked home through the dark city.

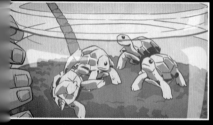

He had four young green turtles with him.

Rats ran around his feet.

Suddenly Splinter saw two men. They had some mutagen

'No one comes to this place,' said one of the men.

They ran after Splinter.

But the mutagen fell over Splinter and the turtles.

'Help!' shouted Splinter and he turned into a rat mutant.

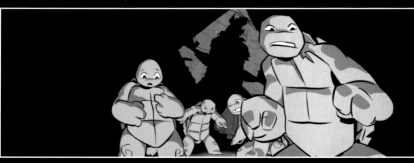

'Aaaarrr!' shouted the young turtles. Now they were mutants too.

Raph went back to the van.

'Who are you?' he asked the man. 'And who makes the mutagen?'

'I'm Snake,' said the man. 'The Kraang make the mutagen. Can I go now?'

'No,' said Raph. 'Take us to the Kraang's lair!'

CHAPTER TWO
The Kraang's lair

Snake took the Turtles to the lair. Leo, Donnie and Raph watched the Kraang from the roof.

'How many Kraangdroids are there?' asked Donnie.

'A lot!' said Leo.

Mikey watched Snake.

'Can I go now?' asked Snake.

'No!' said Mikey.

Mikey came and talked to Leo. 'Hey!' he said.
'I'm hungry. Do you want some pizza?'

Leo looked at him. 'Where's Snake?' he asked.

'He's running away!' shouted Donnie.

'Oh no!' said Mikey.

'Get him!' shouted Leo.

Leo and Raph ran after Snake. Sn[...] the dark.

'Let's drive to the Kraang's lair in S[...] at twelve o'clock!' Leo shouted to R[...]

Snake laughed at the plan. He we[...] Kraang. But Leo and Raph laughed [...] not going to be in the van!' said Le[...]

CHAPTER THREE
Leo's plan

'When do you go?' Splinter asked Leo.

'At twelve o'clock,' Leo answered. 'Do you think it's a good plan, Sensei?'

'Yes,' said Splinter. 'But the Kraang are very strong, and sometimes plans do not work. A good ninja is always ready.'

'Yes, Sensei,' said Leo. 'We are ready.'

At twelve o'clock Snake and the Kraang waited at the lair. They saw Snake's van and they started to shoot.

The Kraang looked in the van ... but no one was there.

The Turtles were on the roof behind the Kraang.

'Quick!' said Leo. 'They can't see us now.'

The Turtles jumped down into the lair.

'Wow!' said Donnie. 'Look at all the computers!'

'Not now!' shouted Raph.

There were Kraangdroids everywhere. The Kraang were strong, but the Turtles were ready.

Raph hit a Kraangdroid and it fell. A pink thing jumped out and ran away.

'What was that?' shouted Raph. 'It was horrible!'

'That was an alien,' said Mikey.

CHAPTER FOUR
'The Kraang are coming!'

Suddenly Donnie saw a door. 'What's in there?' he asked.

It was April and her dad.

'Hi!' said Donnie. 'We're here to help you.'

'Quick!' shouted Raph. 'The Kraang are coming!'

CRASH! Raph hit the door and the Turtles ran into the room. But there was no one there now.

The Kraang had April and her dad. They took them to a helicopter. April was frightened.

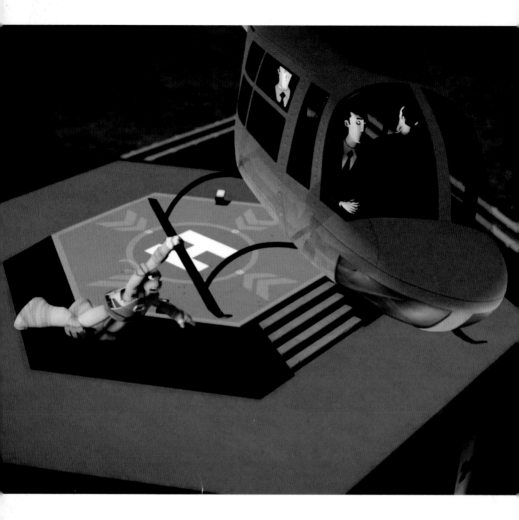

'Donnie, go after them!' shouted Leo.

Donnie jumped up to the helicopter.

'I'm here!' he shouted to April.

A Kraangdroid shot at Donnie. Donnie hit the droid and it fell out. The droid shot again but this time it hit the helicopter.

'Help!' shouted April and she fell out too.

But Donnie was not far behind.

'I've got you!' he said.

Donnie and April watched the helicopter fly away.

'Are you OK?' asked Donnie.

'Yes, thank you,' she said. 'But what about my dad?'

'We're going to find him,' said Donnie.

Leo, Raph and Mikey ran to them. There were more Kraangdroids coming.

'Run!' shouted Mikey.

'Come with us!' Leo said to April.

Splinter waited for the Turtles at home. 'That was good, Leonardo!' he said. 'You stopped the Kraang ... for now.'

But in the dark city the Kraang waited.

THE END

NINJA!

There are many stories about ninjas. The first ninjas lived many years ago, but what do we know about them?

JAPAN

忍者

Watch, think, attack

The first ninjas lived hundreds of years ago in Japan. Ninjas were spies. Ninjas didn't always attack. They were good at watching and thinking too.

Run away and hide

Ninjas were very good at hiding. Sometimes they used smoke. The enemy saw the smoke, and the ninjas had time to run away.

smoke

Stay in the dark

Ninjas did not always wear black. But they went out at night or stayed in the dark. They were very good at staying quiet. They didn't want the enemy to see them. Ninjas were quick and strong. They climbed onto roofs of houses. They watched the enemy from there.

Did you know?
Some ninjas were women. Their name was *kunoichi*.

Do you want to think like a ninja? Do you want to be quick and strong? You can go to ninjutsu classes with a sensei.

★
What can ninjas do? How many things can you find?
★

What do these words mean? Find out.
spy   hide   use   enemy   climb

After you read

1 Who do these sentences describe? Write T for Turtles, K for the Kraang or TK for both.

a) They live in Kraangdroids. — K

b) They live under New York City. — ☐

c) There are four of them. — ☐

d) They make mutagen. — ☐

e) Snake works for them. — ☐

f) They are strong. — ☐

2 True (✔) or False (✗)? Write in the box.

a) The Turtles wanted to find April. — ✔

b) Raph stopped the van. — ☐

c) Snake took the Turtles to the Kraang's lair. — ☐

d) Mikey had some pizza. — ☐

e) There were not a lot of Kraangdroids. — ☐

f) The Turtles and April ran away from the Kraangdroids. — ☐

Where's the popcorn?
Look in your book.
Can you find it?

28

Puzzle time!

1a Write the numbers.

a) There are ..four.. Turtles.

b) Splinter turned into a rat .... years ago.

c) There are .... points on a ninja star.

d) Splinter has .... arms.

e) Raph and Mikey both have two eyes and that makes .... eyes.

f) There is .... Kraang in every Kraangdroid.

b Now add all the numbers and write the total in this sentence.

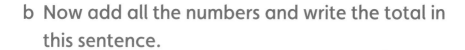

There is a small turtle on page .... of this book.

Are you right? Look and check!

2a Answer the questions.
Who's your favourite character in the story?
Do you like the ending?

b Now ask two friends.

3 Write the words in the crossword. What word do the letters spell? Draw it!

Imagine...

1 Work in small groups. Write a dialogue.
   Use the words and pictures to help you.

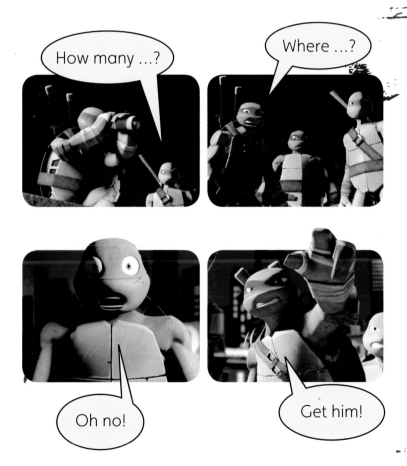

2 Act out your dialogue for your friends.

Chant

1 🎧 **Listen and read.**

Kraang attack!

The Turtles are ready,
Leonardo has a plan.
Go, Turtles!
It's the Kraang attack!

From the roof to the lair,
There are Kraang everywhere.
Go, Turtles!
It's the Kraang attack!

The Kraang have April,
But the Turtles take her back.
Go, Turtles!
It's the Kraang attack!

2 🎧 **Say the chant.**